TAME YOUR MANNERS

AT K.A.M.P.™ SAFARI

K.A.M.P.™ (Kids' Animals & Manners Program)

By Loretta Neff

Founder, The Elegant Way® Foundation

Illustrated by Anirban Mitra

AuthorHouse™
1663 Liberty Drive
Bloomington, IN 47403
www.authorhouse.com
Phone: 1-800-839-8640

Printed in the United States by Bookmasters
Ashland, OH
February 2014
Job Number: 50002367

Published by AuthorHouse 01/28/2014

ISBN: 978-1-4918-2983-7 (sc)
ISBN: 978-1-4918-2984-4 (e)

Library of Congress Control Number: 2013921312

authorHOUSE®

Contents

Images

Introduction: A Note to Parents, Caregivers, and Teachers

With the demanding schedules of parents, caregivers, and teachers, the importance of social skills is often overlooked. Learning social skills early, especially during childhood, can shape a child's character and greatly impact his or her life.

The Elegant Way (EW) Foundation's vision is to teach, inspire, and motivate children to perform spontaneous acts of kindness and consideration and receive the benefits: "to do well by doing good deeds."

The topics covered in this book are part of the EW Foundation's K.A.M.P.™ curriculum.

Tame Your Manners makes manners fun, meaningful, and most importantly, memorable. Any adult or child who reads this book will delight in the clever illustrations and correlations of animal characteristics to the manners advice.

Phrases like "Lions don't need to roar," "Don't be a whino rhino," and "Stand tall like a giraffe" will be forever fixed in a reader's mind.

You're Invited: An African Safari Invitation for Fun, Adventurous Children

Please join me on an African safari! Together we can take a wild ride across the African savanna, journey into the jungle, set up K.A.M.P.™, and be amazed by the beauty of all the majestic creatures of the animal kingdom.

But before we go exploring, there are a few rules that will add to the enjoyment of others (our safari corangers) and ourselves and keep us safe on our safari expedition. A grand adventure and knowledge await us!

It's a Jungle Out There!

Regal Behavior and Rules of the Jungle

- Like a giraffe, stand tall, introduce yourself confidently, and address others with titles of respect.
- With dignity, use your best table manners and honor special guests such as the penguins of Antarctica.
- With a lion's heart, exhibit regal behavior and show the spirit of giving and receiving gifts with humility.
- Like a lemur, treat others with respect and show respect for yourself.
- Be a responsible hyena in the home, an obedient monkey in the classroom, a compassionate hippo on the playground, and a patient rhino in public.
- Have a winning attitude and show the good sportsmanship of a zebra in anything you do.
- Like a grateful elephant, show gratitude and write thank-you notes with sincerity.
- Move as gracefully as a gazelle by putting your best foot forward with a basic box step.

Giraffes

"Poise and Confidence"

Social Introductions

Stand tall like a giraffe and greet with poise, posture, and confidence!

With their remarkable height, giraffes can look far out over the African savanna without having to stand on their tiptoes. Their necks and legs are all about six feet long! With such great height, giraffes have excellent poise and posture.

When you see people you know, greetings are easy, like when you see a fellow classmate from school or a neighbor or when your grandma or grandpa visits. But what about the times you meet a new teacher, someone else's parents for the first time, or new people at school or camp?

Meeting new people and introducing yourself can be scary, but it is well worth giving your best try. Don't worry. New introductions are easy and should not be scary. With a little practice, I'm sure you'll agree.

Introduce yourself with confidence!
- Stand tall like a giraffe.
- Smile! Smiling is the best way to receive a smile in return. It's contagious just like laughing. A smile is also the shortest distance between two people.
- Look the person in the eye. It shows you're sincere and interested.
- Speak with confidence; say your first and last name loudly and proudly without yelling.
- Out of the more than one million words in the English language, try not to use sloppy words like *huh*, *um*, and *eh*.
- Use titles (honorifics) such as Mr., Mrs., Ms., Dr., and Coach for parents, teachers, dentists, doctors, and coaches.
- A conversation is like a tennis match; take turns talking and then listening, and never interrupt.

Penguins

"Dignity and Honor"

Table Manners

Penguins, as guests of honor, receive the royal safari treatment.

Penguins of Antarctica are loyal companions and great at making and keeping friendships.

They have powerful flippers and sleek bodies, which make them incredibly fast swimmers; they can swim as fast as twenty miles per hour. Penguins leap out of the water with sheer joy after they have had a fantastic swim.

Unfortunately, because the environment can at times be unfriendly to the penguins' habitats, they are also considered an endangered species. If we want this bird family to live forever, they need to be given special treatment. Let's do our part and invite the penguins of Antarctica to dinner as guests of honor and give them the royal safari treatment!

Let's have excellent table manners as we welcome our special guests!
- Tiptoe through the safari camp on your way to the table; don't run as if you are part of a herd of elephants!
- Penguins, as guests of honor, sit at the head of the table.
- Put your napkin on your lap immediately after you are seated.
- Guests of honor are served first, females second, males third, and the host or hostess last.
- Wait until everyone is served before you start eating.
- Add something to the conversation about your day or ask about someone else's day.
- Pass serving dishes to the right, keeping hands away from the food.
- Use a clean piece of silverware to scoop dipping sauces onto your plate.
- Tear your bread or rolls into small pieces before applying butter, peanut butter, preserves, or other yummy stuff.
- Use the serving dishes provided.
- Always say, "Excuse my reach," when getting food from a serving bowl.

- Finger foods such as french fries or raw carrots and celery sticks are okay to pick up from the plate with your hands. Or you may use your silverware.
- Tear your straw wrapper with your fingers; don't force it onto the table. No blowing bubbles in your beverage either.
- Bring your glass and food to your mouth; don't hunch over to reach them.
- If you still have food in your mouth, finish chewing and swallow before talking or taking a drink.
- Cut your food, not the plate underneath it.
- Keep your elbows off the table.
- Rest your silverware while you chew.
- Chew your food with your mouth closed.
- Tip your spoon soup away from you when eating soup. When finished, place your spoon on the saucer if one is provided; otherwise, rest it in the bowl. Reminder verse: *"Like little canoes that go out to sea, I spoon my soup away from me."*
- Pat your mouth with your napkin; don't wipe.
- Excuse yourself from the table if you need to use the restroom or blow your nose. Don't use the napkin to blow your nose.
- Place your napkin on your chair or to the left of your plate when you leave the table during a meal; both ways are correct.

- When you are finished eating, wait until plates are removed; don't stack them in a pile.
- When you are finished with your meal, place your silverware on a slant at the four o'clock position.

- Place your napkin to the left of your place setting when you're finished eating.
- Ask to be excused from the table when everyone is finished eating.
- When your special guests are ready to leave, you should accompany them to the exit and say, "Good-bye. Thank you for coming."

"Graciousness"

Lions

"Courage and Humility"

The Spirit of Giving and Receiving

Be gracious and always exhibit the regal behavior of the lion.

Lions are "cool cats." They are proud and brave, and they live in large groups called prides. Lions are very self-confident and know they are "kings of the jungle" and don't need to roar, brag, boast, or bully.

Lions always exhibit regal behavior, unless they're confronted with danger. When in danger, lions roar like thunder—a roar that can be heard from as far as five miles away!

With so many birthdays, holidays, and celebrations every year, it's easy to get excited. Don't just enjoy all the fun and forget to do the right things when celebrating. Whether you are giving or receiving a gift, you should always show (exhibit) the regal behavior of a lion.

Be lionhearted when giving or receiving gifts!
- Be gracious and receive all gifts, big or small, store-bought or homemade, in the same manner so that no one has his or her feelings hurt.
- Do not brag or boast about a gift you're giving or receiving. Do not talk about how much a gift costs.
- Say thank you and show joy with your facial expression and behavior, even if the gift isn't as you hoped or at the top of your wish list.

- Sharing a gift that can be shared, such as a game or food, is a Golden Deed.
- If you receive any gift, especially a gift through the mail from your aunt, uncle, grandparent, or friend, you will get high praises for writing and sending a thank-you note. Good deeds don't go unnoticed, and there's no limit to how many you can do! So go wild and write lots of notes. People like receiving them!

Be regal and generously give a gift!
- On birthdays
- For Mother's Day and Father's Day
- For Teacher Appreciation Day
- When you are attending a sleepover or slumber party
- Just to say thank you

Lemurs

"Courtesy and Respect"

Having Respect for Others and Yourself

*Lemurs treat others with respect and take pride
in themselves and their habitat.*

Lemurs have long pointed noses and bushy tails that they use to communicate with each other. They are very friendly animals and live together in groups. For fun, lemurs like to take turns jumping from tree to tree to play with each other.

Lemurs always treat each other with kindness, courtesy, and respect. They also know that the more respect one gives, the more respect one receives in return. Lemurs take turns with household chores and cleanup, making meals, and doing the dishes. They all do their part to be helpful and respectful in caring for their habitat. Home sweet home.

Showing respect to someone means you act in a way that shows you care about his or her feelings. This includes treating people with courtesy and politeness, being flexible and friendly, and not calling people mean names.

Respect also means caring enough about yourself not to do things that can be harmful to yourself and making sure your own behavior is a good example for others (considering others first). Some examples include not allowing someone or a group of individuals to pressure you into doing something you know is wrong and showing good manners toward others, which tells others that you respect yourself and them too.

Respect is a value that applies at home or school; on the playground or school bus; or in public places like an auditorium, gymnasium, or theater.

It is also important to show respect for someone else's space and things.
- Do not snoop or ask personal or nosy questions.
- Return anything you use in as good or better shape than you found it.
- Be careful not to damage anything that doesn't belong to you.

Keeping a bright, cheery attitude, being considerate of others, and using magic words such as *please, thank you, you're welcome, excuse me,* and *I'm sorry* will ensure that you will do well in life (and master the jungle!)

Hyenas

"Awareness and Responsibility"

How to Be Gracious in the Home

Don't be a wild, loud laughing hyena...
unless doing so won't disturb others!

Hyenas have shorter back legs and longer front legs, which is why they look humpbacked. They also have spots similar to those of Dalmatians.

Hyenas are social animals that communicate with one another through specific calls and signals. They make a lot of curious noises, one of which sounds like laughter. This is the reason they are often called "laughing hyenas." They can be very loud, especially when there is a big group gathered. Hyenas could be considered a nuisance because they are so loud. Have you ever been called a laughing hyena?

Whether you are a guest in someone's home or you have friends coming to your house to visit, do the right thing. Don't be a loud laughing hyena and turn into an unwelcome houseguest.

Be gracious when you have friends at your house!
- Take your shoes off at the door and put away your coat.
- Always use your indoor voice.
- Share your toys and games; sharing is a Golden Deed.
- After everyone has finished eating, ask to be excused from the table.
- Carry your dishes to the sink and offer to help with the cleanup. The faster the cleanup, the sooner dessert comes!
- Pay attention and enjoy your company when you have visitors. Ask questions and listen to the answers. If you use a Game Boy or play a game on the computer, be sure it includes everyone. Use your cell phone only when it's important. Your attention should stay on your guests.

- Keep the bathroom neat and tidy by putting your toothbrush and toothpaste away and hanging towels back on the towel bar.

Be gracious when you go over to a friend's house!
- When staying over at someone else's house, a gracious overnight guest might ask the friend's parent or guardian for permission to bring one of the following gifts to be shared:
- Finger and munch-type foods like popcorn, candies, desserts, and pizza
- Family-oriented games or recreation items such as tickets to the movies, a museum, miniature golf, an amusement park, a sporting event, or a musical show

Monkeys

"Knowledge and Obedience"

How to Be Gracious in the Classroom

*To be as smart as monkeys, pay attention
and don't monkey around in class!*

Monkeys are the smartest animals in all the jungle. They travel in groups called troops or tribes and are seldom seen alone. Because monkeys personally interact so much with each other, they respectfully abide by the common rules to get along with one another and create harmony in their troops.

Monkeys also know how to get down to business and pay attention in the classroom. The reason monkeys are so smart is because they obey the rules, prepare for class, take notes, and listen carefully to the teacher. Because of their obedience and dedication, monkeys become very knowledgeable on many subjects over time. With their high intelligence, well-behaved monkeys know to save "monkeying around" for the playground.

Caring for others and obeying the rules will help you get along with your classmates and teachers and may even help you achieve better grades.

Obey the rules and reap the rewards!
- Show respect for classmates, teachers, and school staff.
- Show respect for the rules that have been put in place for your comfort and safety.
- Respect classroom materials such as books, art and lab supplies, papers, and handouts.

- Pick up after yourself. Throw any trash such as plastic wrappers and cups into a trash container, not on the floor.
- Respect your surroundings. Do not touch or mark on displays or banners or put your feet up on top of chairs.
- Keep your desk tidy. Nobody wants to live in a messy space!
- Practice patience, raise your hand, and wait to be called upon. Your turn will come soon. A classroom of students all speaking at the same time can seem like a loud troop of monkeys!
- Use please and thank-you when asking for something.
- Offer to share what you have with others when possible. Sharing shows caring!
- Learn or take part in new activities like a math or science club, choir, band, or a sport. Learning is a great part of growing up!

Hippos

"Compassion and Loyalty"

How to Be Gracious on the Playground

Make everyone feel special. Don't be a hippo-crite!

Hippos are found in Africa and are the third largest land animal in the world. They have short legs, huge mouths, and bodies shaped like barrels.

Hippos spend a lot of time floating and playing in rivers, lakes, and swamps. They also cherish all different kinds of playmates—clownfish, pink flamingos, and even crocodiles. Hippos are loyal and make everyone feel special by inviting everyone to swim and play along with them.

One thing you never want to be is a hippo-crite (hypocrite), which is someone who acts differently from what he or she says. The best way to make and keep friends is to always treat people as you would like to be treated. You will have many more friendships living by this Golden Rule.

Bullying seems to happen often in the cafeteria and on school buses and playgrounds. Watch out for friends who might need your aid. Stand up for others who need your help and may not be able to stand up for themselves.

Like a hippo, be compassionate and cherish everyone!
- Do not gossip or tell lies.
- Do not play favorites.
- Accept and honor one another's differences and uniqueness; don't poke fun at the wonderful things that make us individually special.
- Do not name-call or tease others.
- Do not pinch, push, or use other kinds of roughness.
- Make everyone feel special and included.

Rhinos

"Patience and Understanding"

How to Be Gracious in Public Places

Be patient and understanding. Don't be a whino rhino!

There are two types of rhinoceros found in Africa—the black rhino and the white rhino—but they are both gray in color. They have thick but sensitive skin and sunburn very easily. To cool and protect their skin, rhinos love to roll and splash around in the mud, which is a natural sunscreen!

Unfortunately, rhinos are also known to have short tempers, and they squeak, snort, and bellow when they don't get what they want. They can also become very cranky when they get sunburned from not protecting their skin.

In life it's not possible to always get what you want when you want it. It's better to learn patience and understanding early in life so you will be better able to adjust in the future and not become so disappointed.

Your parents are right when they say, "Patience is a virtue" (a good thing). You don't want to act like a moody rhino and throw temper tantrums. Take your manners with you wherever you go.

Practice patience and receive praise from parents and teachers!
- Wait patiently in lines—no fussing or complaining.
- Hold doors open for older people (like grandparents), people with babies, people carrying large bags, or people who just need a little extra help.
- Do not complain or distract your parents when they are driving, even if you're excited about your trip.

Zebras

"Integrity and Good Sportsmanship"

Sportsmanship

Like a zebra, you can't change your stripes. So
make sure they're all good stripes!

Zebras travel along the African savanna in groups called herds. They look a lot like horses but have bold black and white stripes. Some zebras have narrow stripes, and some have wider stripes, but they are *all* good stripes.

Zebras and blue wildebeests can be found grazing (eating grass) together. In fact, blue wildebeests rely on zebras to eat the tall grass so they can eat the newly exposed and more nutritious short grasses. The way they take turns eating grass is an excellent example of teamwork. Zebras and wildebeests work together to become most valuable players (MVPs) and achieve a win-win outcome. As a result, they have one of the best teams in all the jungle!

Without saying a word, they show that they have great character and all good stripes by working together in this sportsmanlike way.

Our behavior is more important than what we say or what we look like. Your deeds (what you do) are what people remember, so be sure those memories are good ones. Legendary basketball coach John Wooden once said, "What you are as a person is far more important than what you are as a basketball player." This means that if you're not a nice person, it doesn't matter how well you play a sport or an instrument. Being someone who is not selfish and who helps and pleases others is more important. Also, the goodness of your heart will be remembered long after the game or recital has ended.

By behaving well in tough situations, you may also be rewarded by your coaches and instructors and become an MVP of the team. And when a team has a lot of MVPs, it becomes the best team in the jungle!

Sportsmanship—show the goodness of your heart!
- Always try your best and keep a positive attitude.
- Eat well and get enough rest to make sure you don't become tired and cranky.
- Be honest with the rules.
- Keep your cool even if things don't go your way.
- If you win, it's okay to show excitement, but don't brag or boast.
- If you lose, it's okay to be disappointed, but don't pout, mouth off, or throw objects.
- If you lose, congratulate your opponent with respect.

Elephants

"Gratitude and Sincerity"

Occasions to Write Thank-You Notes

*An elephant would never forget to show gratitude
and thank the ones he or she loves!*

The African elephant is the largest and strongest land mammal on Earth. Elephants show sincerity by forming deep family bonds and living in tight social units.

Elephants are grateful to have tusks that help them peel bark from trees, dig for roots, herd young, and drill for water; trunks that enable them to bathe, communicate, and gather food and water; and large floppy ears with which to fan themselves and cool their bodies.

But best of all, elephants have keen memories that never let them forget to write their thank-you notes! A handwritten thank-you note is thought to be the highest expression of courtesy and respect, and it's something that can last forever and can even become a keepsake.

Show your sincerity and gratitude with a special note!
- When something thoughtful has been done for you
- When you have received a gift
- Just because you feel like it

Thank-You Note Example

Dear _____,

I would like to thank you for _____.

It was a great gift and very thoughtful too!

Your _____,

_____

Gazelles

"Agility and Grace"

Ballroom Dance Lesson

No one in the jungle dances more gracefully than the gazelle!

Gazelles are part of the antelope family. They are known for their speed and grace. They can reach speeds of forty miles per hour, which is as fast as some cars go through town.

When gazelles run, they can jump into the air with all four feet off the ground. When gazelles leap like this, it is called pronking or stotting. Their graceful movements resemble the elegant dance movements of a fox-trot or waltz. In fact, no one in the jungle dances more gracefully than the gazelle!

You too can learn to dance gracefully and put your best foot forward by knowing how to dance the fox-trot.

The Box Step–Fox-Trot

Kings of the Jungle (Boys)
- Step forward with the left foot (count 1).
- Brush right foot to the left foot (count 2).
- Step to the side with the right foot (count 3).
- Close the left foot to the right foot (count 4).
- Step back with the right foot (count 1).
- Brush the left foot to the right foot (count 2).
- Step to the side with the left foot (count 3).
- Close the right foot to the left foot (count 4).

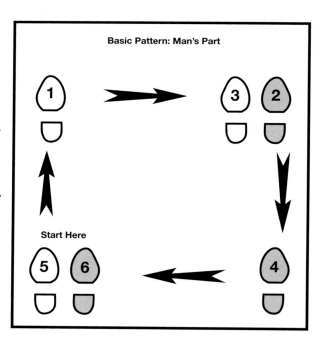

Basic Pattern: Man's Part

Safari Queens (Girls)

- Step back with the right foot (count 1).
- Brush the left foot to the right foot (count 2).
- Step to the side with the left foot (count 3).
- Close the right foot to the left foot (count 4).
- Step forward with the left foot (count 1).
- Brush right foot to the left foot (count 2).
- Step to the side with the right foot (count 3).
- Close the left foot to the right foot (count 4).

Practice Tip

Create a square (roughly twelve by twelve inches for kids and eighteen by eighteen inches for young adults) on the floor with masking tape and softly repeat the rhythm, "Slow, quick, quick, slow" as you take your steps. "Fly Me to the Moon" and "Moon River" are songs that have perfect beats to practice these steps.

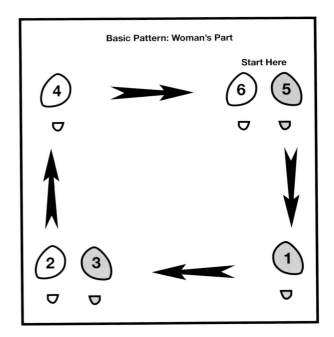

Basic Pattern: Woman's Part

Start Here

Ready for Takeoff!

With the life skills you've learned, you are ready for new and exciting adventures!

By understanding the regal behavior and the rules of the jungle, you will know how to act in all kinds of ways:

- You can stand tall like a giraffe and introduce yourself confidently and address others with titles of respect.
- With dignity, you know how to use your best table manners and honor special guests such as the penguins of Antarctica.
- With a lion's heart, you have learned the spirit of giving and receiving gifts with humility.
- Like a lemur, you understand the importance of treating others with respect as well as showing respect for yourself.
- You know how to be a responsible hyena in the home, an obedient monkey in the classroom, a compassionate hippo on the playground, and a patient rhino in public.
- You will always have a winning attitude and show the good sportsmanship of a zebra in anything you do.
- Like a grateful elephant, you know how to and when it's important to write thank-you notes with sincerity.
- And … when the occasion happens, you can even put your best foot forward with a basic box step and move as gracefully as a gazelle.

Bon voyage!

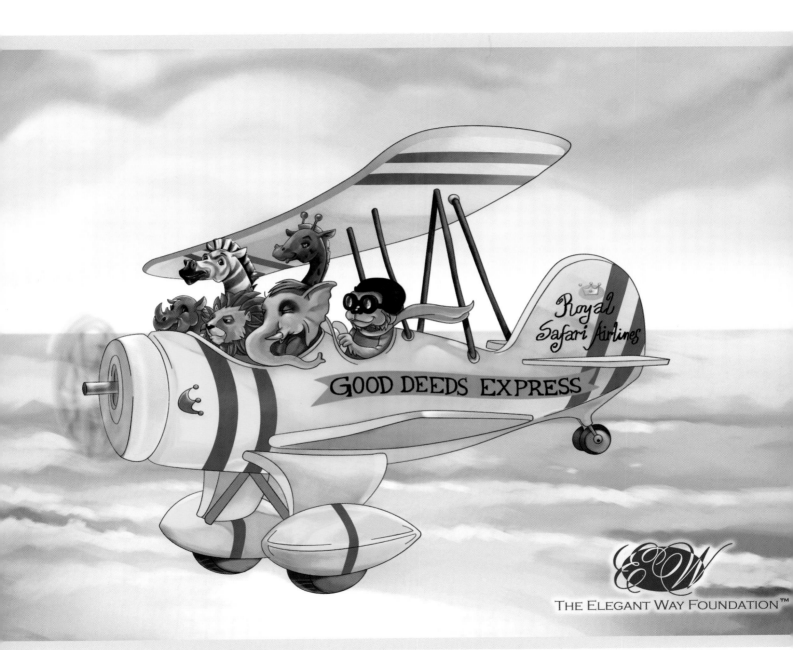

"Determination and Enthusiasm"

The EWF Motto

"Doing well by doing good deeds."

EWF Core Values

Agility–Keeping your mind and body healthy and fit.

Awareness–Thinking of others first; paying attention to your surroundings.

Compassion–Being kind and showing you care about others.

Confidence–Being sure of yourself and having no doubts.

Courtesy–Behaving in a nice manner.

Determination–Doing something and not giving up, even if it's difficult.

Dignity–Having respect for yourself.

Enthusiasm–Being cheerful and always looking for the best in others and every situation.

Graciousness–Being charming and doing nice gestures or good deeds.

Gratitude–Being thankful and feeling blessed.

Honor–Giving special care and attention to something or someone.

Humility–Being self-confident and not bragging or boasting.

Integrity–Being courageous and doing what is right regardless of the outcome.

Kindness–Being warm-hearted and nice.

Knowledge–Becoming educated and learning valuable lessons and skills.

Loyalty–Being faithful and showing you are committed to something or someone.

Obedience–Respecting and following the rules.

Patience–Learning to wait for something or someone without complaining.

Poise–Holding your head up and your shoulders back when sitting and standing.

Respect–How you feel about someone or how you treat someone.

Responsibility–Fulfilling a duty to other people or yourself.

Sincerity–Telling the truth and showing true feelings.

Sportsmanship–Having a good attitude, win or lose.

Understanding–Accepting that others may have beliefs or opinions different from your own.

Glossary

Africa–The world's second largest and second most populous continent. It is located south of Europe and between the Atlantic and Indian oceans.

Antarctica–The continent mostly covered in ice and surrounding the South Pole, which makes it a perfect home for penguins and seals.

Golden Deed–Doing a chore or being responsible for something without being reminded, such as putting your toys and games away or brushing your teeth after a meal.

Golden Rule, the–Treat others as you would want them to treat you, or "Do unto others as you would have them do unto you."

good deed–Doing something when you are asked to do it, such as your homework or going to bed.

honorific–A title or word used to address adults and show respect.

hypocrite (Hippo-crite)–A person who acts in conflict with or differently than his or her stated beliefs or feelings.

K.A.M.P.™ (Kids' Animals & Manners Program, Kids' Arts & Manners Program, and Kids' Athletics & Manners Program) - A unique "edu-tainment" program of inspiring interactive lessons that teaches children self-confidence, a social foundation and to do well by doing good deeds.

manners–The thoughtful ways in which we treat others and perform tasks.

regal–Of notable excellence or magnificence; splendid.

rule–A guide for expected conduct or action.

tame–To change from wild to a softened state of behavior; to make gentle and obedient.

Magical Phrases and Words

The following words are magical and have special power. Use them often.

Please–This word is used in requests or questions.

Thank you–Saying this phrase is a polite way to accept a gift, compliment, or kind gesture.

You're welcome–This is a nice way to answer someone who says, "Thank you." It means you were happy to do the favor or kind gesture.

Excuse me–To say this phrase means to make an apology for something.

I'm sorry–Saying this is a way to express regret or sympathy.

The Elegant Way Foundation
Certificate of Achievement

"Doing well by doing good deeds."

My Pledge

I pledge to do my best, exhibit gracious manners, and live by the Golden Rule.

_____

Child's Signature   Date

Quotes of Inspiration

Those who bring sunshine to the lives of others cannot keep it from themselves.
—Sir James M. Barrie (creator of Peter Pan)

True happiness comes from the joy of deeds well done, the zest of creating things new.
—Antoine de Saint-Exupery

So shines a good deed in a weary world.
—William Shakespeare and Willy Wonka

About the Elegant Way Foundation

The Elegant Way Foundation Inc. (EWF) was founded in 2012 by Loretta A. Neff, president of the Elegant Way School of Protocol, as a philanthropic organization to promote manners and civility worldwide through various charities, missions, and schools.

Mission

Our mission is to promote manners and civility by providing educational programs, financial resources, and volunteer support for the benefit of children and young adults.

Vision

Our vision is to empower children and young adults with social tools necessary to succeed in school and beyond, to provide value to our charity partners, and to improve the human condition worldwide.

The Elegant Way Foundation Inc.
561.833.0131
www.theelegantwayfoundation.org
www.tameyourmanners.com

All net proceeds from this book will go to charity. Awaiting nonprofit 501(c)(3) status.

About the Author

Loretta Neff is president of The Elegant Way School of Protocol, a boutique etiquette firm represented in Fort Lauderdale, Naples, and West Palm Beach, Florida.

Loretta received a BA degree in 1989 and had her sights on the legal profession. But after being accepted to Thomas Cooley Law School at Michigan State University, she never attended, having found her real passion to be philanthropy through teaching the social graces.

While living in Cleveland, Ohio, Loretta joined a private club, and it was there that she was first invited to teach dinner manners and social graces to children of other members. From that early experience, referrals segued over the years into a host of other clients, from individuals to Fortune 500 companies, prompting her to sometimes refer to herself as "an accidental entrepreneur." What was to be a postponement of law school became a thriving career–and a driving mission.

Loretta remains committed to the advancement of numerous charities, societies, and educational foundations and has taken her philanthropy to another level with the formation of The Elegant Way Foundation, a nonprofit organization intended to provide resources and training in social skills to other charities, missions, and schools as part of its mission.

Marketing/Promotional Copy

"What a painless way for children to learn proper behavior, helpfulness, courtesy, and character! Wouldn't be surprised if their parents didn't pick up a few tips along the way."
—Dianna Booher, author of *Communicate with Confidence* and *Creating Personal Presence*

"Every young person I know will be getting Tame Your Manners *for his or her next birthday. In fact, I'm getting one for myself!"*
—D. A. Benton, author of *The CEO Difference* and *Lions Don't Need to Roar*

*"*Tame Your Manners *is very clever, cute, and easy to visualize, which will help kids remember these valuable lifetime skills. My son and I think this book is awesome!"*
—Robin Groves, super mom and super athlete